AFTER COLONNA

ANNA KEY

AFTER COLONNA

Contemporary Devotional Sonnets

IN THE WIND
projects

Cover Image: G. Rymer, *A View of Delphos and Mount Parnassus*, lithograph,1832
(Public Domain Image)

Based aboard Sailing Vessel *Blowin' in the Wind,*
In the Wind Projects is a multimedia collaborative committed to ways of thinking, working and living that go beyond the closed room.

In the Wind Projects
411 Walnut Street #12918
Green Cove Springs, FL 32043

inthewindprojects.org

ISBN: 978-1-949497-03-8

CONTENTS

FOREWORD

These sonnets were written using Vittoria Colonna's *Sonnets for Michelangelo* as a spiritual exercise. I tried, sonnet for sonnet, to find in myself the spiritual movement that gave rise to the sonnet, and then to write from that place, to feel the urgency and the difficulty of it. At the beginning, I almost wanted to translate them, to stay very close to Colonna's images and ideas; as the project developed, I began to think of my sonnets as "recompositions" of hers: related, but different. In the end, it became clear that however indebted my sonnets are to hers, and however impossible it would have been to write them without Colonna as my guide, what emerged is something wholly unexpected and new.

ACKNOWLEDGMENTS

Portions of this manuscript have appeared in the following publications: sonnets 1, 2, 9 and 18 in *Dappled Things*; sonnets 21 and 25 in *The Windhover*; sonnets 23 and 29 in *Amethyst Review*; sonnets 86 and 100 in *Catholic Poetry Room*, sonnets 4, 9, 31 and 41 in *Convivium*; and sonnets 51 and 58 in *Evangelization and Culture*.

This project would not have been possible without the admirable effort of Abigail Brundin, whose searching translation of Vittoria Colonna's *Sonnets for Michelangelo* helped guide me through the Italian, and whose words occasionally drift into my sonnets. I am grateful for her work and for her guardianship of Colonna's sonnets, which do not deserve to be consigned to the realm of those many ingenious lovely things that are gone.

AFTER COLONNA

1

All I wanted after love left me was fame.
I can't recall now what I hoped to find—
lust grew like a snake in my gardened mind
until love turned to blame, and blame, more blame.
Let me write with nails your holy name;
your blood my ink, make me patient and kind;
let my words be on your lifeless body signed
that others may know you suffered, you came.
Why would I invoke Delos or Parnassus?
You're the only island I long to reach,
the only mountain I ever hope to climb.
Let your sun shine on me as it passes us;
let it warm me, enlighten me, and teach
me, Lord, to find your truth in humble rhyme.

2

I want to walk behind you, Lord, up that
impossible path, cross on my back, all
light streaming from you. Only when I fall
will I see what Peter saw, and say what
he said, when he alone knew you. I thought
I could hope this on my own, but I'm small;
by your light alone find the door in the wall;
every human hope is made of glass, but
yours remains. O God, generous and sincere,
if I could come to your table, all my
desire for your food alone, all other
desires being gone, I might be here,
fully present and full, ready to die
beside you, in the arms of your sweet mother.

3

I want to look at it, to understand,
the way I want to see and know the sun;
but its fire remains unseen, my thoughts undone
by the blinding light of true God and true man.
Still, who would think this changing light could span
a universe of darkness, warming one
whose cold hope had long been on the run?
Like a ray, he reaches out his wounded hand
and unburdens worthless burdens of the world,
then yokes my neck, gently, with his true yoke
to lead me home. In the beautiful clear
light I see my hidden, sinful heart pearled
by humility, that sweet word he spoke
which unlocks all the others. Lord, let me hear.

4

Abyss of true light, immense and pure, you
turn your kind and loving eyes toward us, we
who crawl about the world like ants, not free
but worldly-wise and hard of heart. Undo
the hurtful wall of ignorance that grew
like the lengthening shadow, cold and darkly,
of the old Adam—impious enemy
of your warm rays, clear and sure and new.
O God my God, clothe us with living faith and
loving fire; fold your law into our hearts like
leaven; teach us to fly, to leave behind
selfish desire, caught in itself like a lake.
Beyond it, where we lightly go, your hand
hands us the key your sweet gates to unlock.

5

If I set before my small soul all of
God's life-giving graces, I think I should
fall like a raindrop into that all-good
sea, wholly absorbed by oceanic love.
And falling into that eternal wave,
surfing swiftly from joy to joy, I would
feel the smallness of what solid stood
and death and all luck, good or bad, I might have.
And holding fast to great ideals of youth,
to ardent love for oceans, rivers, mountains,
I'd feel the freeing rays of falling sun
fall all around like bright liquid fountains
that transform the world and hard hearts of men,
disperse the shadows and demonstrate the truth.

6

I wish that I could trust you more, who feed
the birds and clothe the lilies, but I'm still
full of hope for the wrong thing, and my weak will
still worries about all I want and need.
Could I but hurt and suffer, want and bleed
with joy, keeping my eyes fixed on that sweet hill
where your opened side opened to me, hell
might reveal its heaven and heaven, hell. Lord,
this is the light you shine into my darkness
where I learn to embrace what I avoid,
letting love lead me into poverty
and pain, letting go of all I vied
to gain, standing before God in pure starkness
against a pale sky, like a leafless tree.

7

My angelic escort, sent to me by
God, guide my mind along the straight path to
heaven; and when I stumble, as I do,
help me to see God as you do, with high
hope and humble knowing. I don't know why
I so often think myself alone, with few
who understand me, or care what is true,
when you are here, who know, and care, and try.
When all this darkness is all almost gone,
and my time of suffering is almost done,
lead me like the birds to sing out my song
and trust that the waiting will not be long;
show me the signs, like an internal dawn
of the coming of my bright and blessed sun.

8

The waters of a world searching in vain
against God taste so bitter, full of fear
and hate and hidden things that disappear
beneath a clouded surface and are gone
from view, but still felt, and feared. With what strain
we twist and turn ourselves year after year,
trying to unfeel the pull, to unhear
the call to waters that could heal all pain.
They roll in, broad and clear, powerful and true,
their crystalline secret revealed to all
who humble themselves to enter that wild
green chamber, elegant and fierce and mild,
which carries us beyond ourselves and through,
leading and inviting like a moving wall.

9

Today she was born who gave birth to God;
time wound and unwound in her sacred womb
where she became what she was before, loom
upon which eternity was woven. Guide
me, Holy Mother, body of light, laud
of angels; like a flower in your room
turn my face toward your sun and make me bloom;
let me stand one bright day loving and unflawed.
So unlike you now, full of spite and rank
impatience, I cry out like a child, loud
and helpless, trying with the few words I
have to let go of all in me that's proud,
to ask of everything I do why and why,
to say, with Peter, I walked before I sank.

10

The window of the soul is hard to keep
clean; from inside and outside, far and near
one must examine every smudge and smear
to try to make the vision clear. It's a steep
ascent that would feel like the sleepless sleep
of Sisyphus, were it not for the dear
promise of its end and the sweet hope, here
and now, that it's still possible to leap.
It's God's image in the glass, like seeing
a world in front of you reflected from
behind, but no less real, a world of light
that children instinctively know is Being
and pass freely into and turn to welcome
any who would look and see with their pure sight.

11

I eat food and it becomes part of me,
invisibly, forming and reforming
me out of itself. Like a living, storming
sky fed by invisible forces, we
come to your table and receive what we
can't see, upbuilding sacrament firming
our weak faith, body for body, warming
our cold human reason mercifully
that we might come to know and be as you
know and are. Our knowing is so small, our
pride so stubborn, that we would starve, and do,
before the bread of heaven falling hour
by hour at our feet. Lord, please say you knew
me, that I ate and lived by your power.

12

Time of darkness, waiting for you; time of
darkness, preparing to see; come to me
and find me made for you the way the tree
is made: patient, enduring, rising above.
My night was long and I thought would prove
to be within me, night I could never flee,
blindness from birth, irremediable; but see,
before you come, fully yourself, fully love,
in the fullness of light that day is, you
light for me the little lights of faith and
hope, lights of fire that burn like the sun, though
small; but even small, I know I can see through
the darkness because I can see and know
the way a sailor long at sea sees land.

13

O Lord, you conquered this terrible world
already; all worldliness has already
been undone. Why we go on with petty
designs and worries on this blue ball hurled
through the darkness, I don't know. My soul furled
then unfurled, finding at last a steady
wind to hold onto; I sailed past the jetty
of desire, past blue and gray waters swirled
at the harbor's edge out into the pure
blue crisis. How many ever leave sight
of land? Out here, it seems so few. To feel
this alone, this afraid, this free; assured,
almost, of the soundness of my small boat
and of its bold capacity to heel.

14

If, with Zacchaeus, my need to see you
could send me skittering up a tree, no
regard for what others thought of me, so
absorbed with thoughts of you that I flew
into the branches like a bird and knew
their lightness, for a moment, then below
could stay where it belongs, and I could go
with you, floating on air, seeing the world anew.
Come to my house, Lord, and take shelter; find
here what has been lost and lead me from house
to home that I might be where you are; for
having seen you, Son of Man, my eyes are blind
to anything but you; eternal light, spouse
of my soul, I knock, softly, at your door.

15

I'm angry that you take away my easy
life, all human honor, easy money;
all my desires thwarted, all sunny
days eclipsed and nothing ever breezy;
poor and outcast, the world thinks I've gone crazy;
the world stares and laughs when nothing's funny
while I labor for invisible honey
and the world thinks me useless and lazy.
My God! I love you so imperfectly I
wonder whether I love you at all. My
heart is in limbo, there's still so much to
let go of in order to embrace you. Why
do you leave me alone and broken by
the wayside? Let me, lying here, be true.

16

Arrogance the destroyer, enemy
of all things good and true, where does it come
from? What makes us think we're better than some,
or most, what makes us want to be? In me
it lurks below like a sea anemone
or sits on the surface like a rainbowed film
that poisons everything beneath; other times,
it calls down to itself humble Persephone,
leading me to times of infertility.
I don't know how to avoid its quiet traps,
or how to clean up its oil spill in my mind;
only I have seen sweet humility
in all its springly splendor unwind
the tight bind that haughty winter wraps.

17

From brief poverty great riches, from short
suffering eternal joy; but Lord, how
hard it is to hold onto when from bow
to stern my little boat is tossed about
so violently, and the nearest port
seems impossibly far away, and now
is all I can see, for standing at the prow
my visibility is zero. I shout
out cries and profanities that are torn
from my lips by the wind; do you hear me,
Lord? I don't know how to find peace when all
I can do to survive is work, and crawl
about the deck trying not to get thrown
off. My God, will this storm ever not be?

18

If the heavens gave up a shining light
to set fire to the earth so that it burns
for our salvation, what proud ice unlearns
the fire in our frozen minds so that we fight
against the fire to preserve our cold night?
The body resists the fire and yearns
for comfort, but the searching spirit turns
toward it; how to get the body past spite
to joyful embrace of its decrepit state,
how to suffer pain and want, want and pain
willingly; to learn to give up, to wait;
to trust that all this trouble is not in vain.
Lord, help me hold to the difficult, hate
the easy, commit to fire and strain.

19

Your gift, Lord, is that a mortal being
can attain the infinite; you came down
to die our death that we, wearing your crown,
might share your life. The cross is the door. Seeing
you hanging there, hanging and not fleeing,
though you could, not seeing I would surely drown
in the desperately confused brown
waters of a despairing finitude. Freeing
us from that uncertain sea was a gift
that none could comprehend, but many have
forgotten. Too familiar now, we lay
claim to our finitude and try to lift
ourselves on wings of our own making, heaving
ourselves into a mute sky made of clay.

20

My God, you've made me a living branch on
the broad vine of truth; let my leaves be full
and supple, let them bear good fruit; let cool
breezes move me, let the light of your dawn
shine on me. With tender mercy you have drawn
me to yourself, grafted me with the tool
of grace onto the tree of life. I pull
away, sometimes. I'm sorry. My leaves gone
in winter, I worry that my branches will stay
bare. But you are patient and kind through
many seasons, your goodness rooted in
eternal soil; let the warm light of your ray
draw forth forgiving sap to heal my sin,
send forth fresh green growth and make me new.

21

However much I distrust myself, so
much more must I trust you; for you, bright star,
you illuminate everything. I stare
at the long blades of grass that blow
in your warm wind and admire how they glow
in your warm light; so, too, the waters store
up your light on a thousand waves. I steer
by your saving light alone, there is no
other. When I go into the new-moon
darkness of myself, help me not to get
too lost; teach me not to trust in the frail
power of artificial light, its noon-
day brightness like an anti-sun. Lord, let
me shine with your light, bright and true and real.

22

I often sail through cold and mist toward God's heat
and light, which melt away an ice-age of
proud neglect and let searching waters move
again, making a way for my small boat
to navigate safely toward him. If my heart
remains cold and dark, yet with all my love
I turn toward heaven and deep within have
the sense that I can hear decades of hurt
calving off the glacier of myself; then,
in the profound silence after, I hear
a kind voice say, "Be not afraid, for when
he came into the world, ample and clear
ocean of eternal good, he sent
small, gentle waves to draw the humble near."

23

I wish that the true sun, upon which I
always call, would send an eternal light
into my mind, instead of this weak white
light that undoes my vision; I wish my
heart would go up in flames with your holy fire
instead of warming itself, as at night,
from a safe distance; I wish my weak sight
could fix itself on you alone, Most High,
instead of chasing shadows. If I could
see you, Lord, if I could see you as you
are, then I could stand before you and knit
your bright rays into a garment with true
lines, that my body might shine and be good,
outside brilliant and inside every part lit.

24

What is humility? I would be a proud
fool to say I know. Cherished by God, she
reveals his great mysteries to the peace-
loving heart. She wasn't the virtue espoused
by the ancients; they had many gods, bowed
to love and war, sun and moon, harvest, sea;
but what did their proud gods know of humility?
Then Christ came, quietly, into the loud
world and showed us the least-expected way
to heaven. Lord God, my God! I cry out
to you from within a prison of pride,
walled in by rigid thoughts that bring delay
and keep me from walking through the humble, wide-
open door that leads to a place beyond doubt.

25

The sky, the earth, the sea, each element
renders testimony to the divine cause
everywhere evident in creation. Whose
soul is so divided that a love meant
for heart and mind turns to cold experiment
and warm pose in search of empty applause?
Now wounded earth weeps beneath clouds like gauze,
and the human soul, of heart and mind, is rent.
There is no anti-intellectual love,
nor is the cross the end of mind; and if
we cease to love creation wholly, how
will we be whole or live our love to prove
for the Creator? We're hanging on a cliff
and need the strength of heart and mind right now.

26

I seem to see a woman of passion and
spirit, far from the errant crowd in her
lonely dwelling; and I see her bold turn,
deliberate and true, toward the true land
across the true sea. It was a sea that spanned
unimagined miles, and she was heir
to so much fear. She wiped your feet with her hair
and touched your risen body with her hand
because she knew, as she pushed off the known
shore and began, intensely, to suffer cruel
misunderstandings and isolation, whir
of wind and waves, yet still she knew the one
thing needful was to love you like a fool.
So I dare to pray, *Dear God, make me like her.*

27

I taste and taste and taste, and what I taste
I taste for taste alone. Tongue of my desire,
why do you spurn nature's cleansing bitter
and her time of fast, why do you waste
my life on tea and cakes and ices? Make haste
and shut the gates, they come with stone and fire
to undo the work of the simple friar
who ate dirt and true poverty embraced.
The earth needs us now; he saw the way
to near-perfect reconciliation:
give up everything, and eat in peace
only what is given; fast and pray;
take great joy in the bitter, the plain; ration
what is good until the time of war should cease.

28

He came into the world to gather up
all danger, all violence, all threat, all
fear and to carry it, body and soul,
all in himself, all of it, impossible step
by impossible step. He wanted to stop,
wanted but couldn't because he heard the call
and followed it to the end, fall for fall,
to make a safe way for us. *Lord, take this cup*.
His great love burst forth out of his sacred heart
like bright rays from behind a cloud, thick and low.
He shines and waits. We must have such cold feet
and hearts of stone covered in deep shadow
if in such bright light and intense heat
we do not melt like soft wax or white snow.

29

O my soul, the Lord is coming, now chase
away the mists that surround you with his clear
and holy light. Let it lift doubt and fear
like a blanket of fog from a field; face
his bright sun with humble courage; embrace
the intensity of heat and light which bears
down on us, too hot for comfort, here
struggling in this earthly dwelling place.
It's hard to grow, and hard to change, and hard
to sweat out all the sin and hurt, false desires,
failures and false hopes that course through our proud
veins; but when it's done, my soul, when the fires
have given up their flames and the sun has heard
your cry, God himself will say your name out loud.

30

I miss you is all I can say today;
so much of the world stands between you and
me, and so much of me, the shifting sand
of myself, stands like a desert in the way.
My God, how can I reach you? When you lay
in the manger, immortal God, maker of land
and sea, maker of me, did you reach out your hand
trustingly, was I there, did you call me to stay
by your side like a mother? Could I hold
you now and feel the strength of your knowing?
The road ahead looks like water in this heat;
the logic of the world would be so bold
as to label it illusion; but my feet
trust they'll find the sea, if I just keep going.

31

If the faint sound, which alone stirs and moves
the frail air, stirs and moves me; and the breeze
gathers up the pieces of me, gently, and frees
my mind from the world's seductive grooves
to say in a weak whisper, *Love proves*
itself in weakness; if I am seized
with love for you when I hear you in the trees
and fall to my knees alone, all other loves
being gone; what then will my weak heart do
when my inner ear hears your soft voice spoken
in the quiet music of the sky, which told
and still tells of a world wholly true
where the steady rhythm is never broken
and the heavenly sound never grows old?

32

Behind your great captain, your divine king,
you followed bravely, finding yourself heir
to bitter struggles and the blank cruel stare
of a world that sought, and so found, nothing.
You had everything to give and gave everything;
your cross your only treasure, you laid bare
your soul to the unfeeling world whose care
was always elsewhere; and you felt the sting,
felt it deeply, but it only deepened
your love and your holy resolve. Francis,
be with me now; the world has crushed and cheapened
everything you fought for; its cold, flat expanses
have widened, and the true way has steepened,
and it will take your bold faith to withstand this.

33

Francis, in whom as if in humble wax,
Jesus imprinted his wounds of love; and
stamped thus, like a seal on a letter, he would hand
to the world Christ's message of peace. He walks
lightly on the dry land the way Peter walks
on water; borne up by faith, across sand
and sea, they felt the new earth stirring like a mind
sensing light, once dreaming, stirs and wakes.
The world has almost forgotten that it's
a human dwelling place, because we've lost
all sense of our humanity. Christ came
to show us who we are and to bear the cost
of who we fail to be. My God, in his name,
help us to be human before the whole earth quits.

34

I long for a clear and distinct calling
which my heart pursues with passion, that my
words might shine forth like stars in a night sky
still necessary to find our way by. Walling
ourselves in now, the sky, the stars are falling
and words (words!) rain down hard on a hard, dry
land in muddy rivers, while earth's muffled cry
goes unheard by hearts and minds still stalling.
What are poets for in a destitute time?
Does the blood of the Word run in our veins?
My God, when we have all been forgotten,
like your son, and all earth's gentle rains
have gone, rescue us, Lord, and take us home
to live in and with the Word begotten.

35

I want to be like the saints whose spirits
are never afflicted by time or by toil,
who bear all things with peace and joy, loyal
to the cross to the end. But I can't come near its
still and still moving center, can't hear its
simple song, eternally new. I spoil
everything with complaint and so lose the royal
air of suffering; every day I fear its
coming in the form of pain, or loss, or
sickness, the cruel word or the unkind hand.
I'm tired and worn down, old, unknown and poor,
exhausted in body, mind and spirit; and
I want to love you better, Lord, to give more
than I am; forgive me, Lord, I can hardly stand.

36

I wish that in the harsh, lowering storm
of this tormented world, I could climb aboard
the ark with Noah, safe while the rains poured
down and everything living came to harm;
or else with haste cross through the shocking form
of sea parted from sea and sing to the Lord
on the far shore a joyful song, turned toward
a life in which there's no more need to mourn;
or else with Peter, when I feel my faith
shrinking from the threatening waves, I wish
that I could feel my heart lifted by the divine
hand and walk safely where others sink. Wash
me, Lord, in your saving waters, and draw forth
from my heart waters of truth like fine wine.

37

God called you to a boat, Noah, when all
the world was dry; in their sterile, fierce
aridity, they mocked you like a fool, and worse;
there must have been an easier way, a call
unheard, a willingness to build a wall
around your heart, to join the crowd. Your curse
to be so set apart, like the final pierce
in Christ's sacred body, brought to the fall,
fallen and falling world God's saving grace
in the form of water: a fresh start
in the flood and the font, all darkened trace
of selfishness gone. O my weak and fearful heart,
can you not trust like Noah and turn to face
the rising waters with a courage set apart?

38

It’s hard to think of heaven, and to wonder
whether and if and what; but still somehow
a comfort to trust that time will come, flow
into his wide sea—wide and true and tender—
releasing us from fear of wave and thunder,
of all that could be or fail to be from now
until the hoped-for day when all time will allow
is living in the midst of time to wander.
Time to wander deeper into the heart
of his unknown, and every realm a new
vision of his goodness, and every soul
a reflection of his light, and every part
fitted to his perfect whole. My God, my goal,
help me here and now to belong there, too.

39

God, the true lover, chose to come to earth
in mortal form and took our human error
as his own, a perfect gift, to bear for
us the sins we could not bear ourselves. From birth
he felt our darkness gathering as, from the north,
a winter storm approaches; and our poor
sight looked upon him coldly, not to care or
try to find a way to know him. Our worth
resides in him and him alone, yet still
we look to anything and anyone
else to make us feel we matter. My Lord,
could I but trust you more and myself less, then
I could see what you would have for me and will
to be with you in deed, and thought, and word.

40

The first martyr kept his eyes fixed on God,
not only because his mind was pure and
good, but because every stone thrown by the hand
of his enemy seemed to him a guide
straight into the heart of heaven and a guard
against every impurity. He loved the man
who cast the stone as ardently as any
mother loves her son, for he knew it was a fraud
to think the world could do him any harm;
and no man ever prized a precious gem
more than Stephen prized the stone that pierced straight
through the center of his loving heart. As the stem
of his life bent, then broke, his precious, warm
blood flowed out like red petals, erasing all hate.

41

What am I holding onto, that I should be
so sad? is maybe what he thought leaning
his head upon the breast of our Lord. Meaning,
perhaps, that time seen through is still and only
time, horizon of hurt, betrayal, friendly
fire, of things that go wrong, or seem to; weaning
ourselves off of its comforts and cleaning
the dirty panes of its desires lets us see,
if only a little, beyond the despair
of now. But still things end, painfully, and
goodbyes are still, if not forever, hard
to say; he felt it all, and felt it hard to bear,
and felt in his soul what he couldn't understand;
then gave us the Prologue as our eternal guard.

42

Some hurts run so deep they can't be undone;
and there never was a deeper hurt than
Mary's as she held her dead son and tears ran
down her blessed cheeks. Although the bright sun
shone, and she saw him raised and watched him run
as he had when still a child; and although his plan
grew clearer in her mind, yet still the man
who lay pierced and lifeless was her treasured son.
It was a scene she never could unsee,
a thought she never could unthink, a pain
she never could unfeel. In her faithful mind
she saw the glory and the holy victory;
yet in her pure maternal heart, her slain
son remained a wound time never could unwind.

43

When you saw, Holy Mother, little by
little the light draining from the bright eyes
of your beloved son, I believe your cries
carried you to where he was and let you try
to recover what was dearest in him, Most High,
within your own heart; but your deepest sighs
were borne away by a careless wind, and skies
long lit by his holy light grew dark. *Why?*
must have been a thought you held tight to your
Immaculate Heart; for who could doubt
the immeasurable pain you endured,
for me and for all mankind, to make a door
where sin had made a wall. Holy Mary, without
your healing love, our pain would be assured.

44

Blessed mother, what must it have been like
to bear the son who made you, to hold
the author of the universe in your pale, cold
hands on a cold night where none would think to look?
Your shining secret shining in the dark lake
of the world like a bright star, bright and bold,
reflecting off its surface, the great foretold
at once above and here, come to heal our lack.
At his birth, at his death, when he rose
into heaven, he found you by his side,
comforter, companion, mother complete
and true—a gift to him which he in turn made
a gift to all. Gentle mother, wrap me in your sweet
grace like a babe held tight in swaddling clothes.

45

Luke's virgin is imperfect. His mind so
full of the immensity of his concept,
his painting came forth bit by bit, inept,
perhaps, as some would have it. He had no
flow, no smooth pour, his execution low
and lowly. Possibly he tried, and kept
trying, to make a painting that was more adept,
and left instead a record of his failure. But oh,
it is enough, isn't it, to finish
in humility and failure, having
perfected only what the world can't see?
She is there, full of grace, her only wish
to lead us to God. He loved, and loving
painted the Mother of Love truly.

46

Ursula, the angels swept through the air
like falcons, eleven thousand strong, to bring
to you and your companions, from your king,
the palms and crowns of martyrdom. And where
were you then but far from home, brave girl, there
in a foreign, hostile country seeking
deeper understanding of the truth? Sing
to me now, pilgrim saint, sing of that rare
virtue, courage, so dear to the ancients
but lost, somehow, to modern man; sing of
the search, of the need to travel on earth
to find our way to heaven. Let your entrance
into heaven lead many hence; let us go forth
from our houses in search of our home above.

47

Is it the new earth that I sense when I think
of a place without machines, without waste,
without anything ever done in haste,
without poisonous food and poisonous drink,
without searching hearts and minds on the brink
of total collapse? I thought I could taste
it, once, in an elegant dream that raced
through my mind like a wild horse, like wild pink
ribbons chasing the sun over a hopeful
horizon, which leads to a place we can
attain only by moving. Move us, thou
unmoved mover; move us to be helpful
and kind, to love this broken earth and fallen man,
to feel the pull of heaven here and now.

48

It is coming, the death that will bring an
end to this. It is coming, like rain, like
sun, beloved, life-giving, welcome. I ache
in every part of me, too tired to push on;
but through the fabric of it, like the sun
streaming through threadbare cloth, I look
to the light of what lies beyond and take
what comfort I can in the midst of pain.
It struck me just the other day, walking
down an ordinary street, how beautiful
life is, how astonishing the fact of
my existence in the world; and the bountiful
dream washed over me like rain, like love,
like the joyful sound of people talking.

49

The stable, the animals, the cold, and the hay,
and his poor rags, and his cold bed, all were
a sure sign of his celestial grace; and sure
they came, the three wise kings, they came to pay
homage to their forever king, who lay
swaddled, tiny and poor, under a bright star
burning in a cold sky. They saw him stir,
felt small and alone like him; but the bright ray
of his certain light guided their uncertain
hearts to his. So hard the way, to leave
behind the familiar and the known, unbidden
in the eyes of the world; journey of love
guided by a loving fire hidden
beyond the warm room and closed curtain.

50

Oh little ones, oh Holy Innocents,
oh mothers of mourning, oh blood in the street—
you suffered before them the terrible fate
that would befall them, too, and make no sense
to a world which, in its blindness or arrogance,
no longer believes in the path, short and straight,
to heaven; or in the glorious feat
of Christ on the cross, or the way of penance.
That there is a war here between evil and good,
that we make a choice which side to be on,
that the weapons are never, ever laid down—
who could doubt, who can hear the sorrow of God
in the cries and the silence of the children gone
like unwanted chaff by a violent wind blown?

51

Lady, Our Lady, did you not press and pour
into your milk, like essential oils wrung,
the whole of you, like living breath into lung,
to nourish the whole of your divine son? Or
did his living fire scorch your holy breast, and more,
breaking into pure light and pure song
the pieces of you like a universe born?
Who can understand it, how spirit tore
into the material world like lightning,
did not burn but lit it up in a flash
that lasted through the long night, whitening
like snow the dark, dark world? In the flesh
he came and defied every logic, not frightening
but consoling like the evening's red flush.

52

One fire alone inflamed her, one thought led
her through her days; she never felt the pull
of darkened reason, nor heard the hard, cruel
words of willful confusion. What he said,
those words she heard, and felt in heart and head
the shining purity, the harmonic rule
of a heavenly logic, bright and full,
that came in the flesh, through her, suffered, bled.
My God, my path has been much less straight;
and I am most unworthy of your words.
Have mercy on me now and lead me home
along the path of the prodigal son; late
though he came, yet when he lately heard,
you filled his heart with your heavenly hymn.

53

Clear and sure star of our sea, be with us;
for we are as children, young and afraid,
in need of a mother's hand. Your son made
things possible not possible before; is
it then possible for us to be as
he is, calm on the wild sea, unswayed
of purpose, sure of faith, trusting on the wide
open water that all will be well, and was,
and is? Land seems so far away, and peace,
and rest; and a place to call home is a dream.
Where are you, Lord, and when will you come? We
are lost, we perish, when will the winds cease?
Hear the cry in our hearts, dear Mother, be
our hope that things are not as they seem.

54

I'd like to witness with a pure and noble mind
your war in the heavens, fair angels, who
fought neither with iron nor pride but with true
and sound knowledge of God. Proud they were, and blind,
your enemies; and they labored and pined
after power and riches, though they knew,
and still know, God as you do. It's hard to
understand how perfect knowledge doesn't bind
us, of itself, to truth; but only the will
to love. Love and love alone, freely chosen;
and by virtue of this freedom, sometimes
freely left. Hard to understand, yet still
the turning world turns from the sun, frozen
in a willful winter which from itself stems.

55

Contemplating Christ on the cross, I fell
on my face and wept; for it is my sin
that placed him there. I knew it, fiercely, then
and know it still. For the bottomless well
of concupiscence draws, daily, toward hell,
at least a little, and again and again,
even the heart fixed firmly in love of him.
So we go, again and again, go and tell
with humble and penitent hearts how we
have failed; and through his priests, he listens
and forgives. It is no easy road, this;
not easy to fall and fall again, to carry
the cross unto death; but the tear glistens
like a gem in the crown of eternal bliss.

56

I’m tired, Lord. But still the ancient fear
of death crowds me, and makes me long for space.
Space to run, to fly, to trust; to feel my place
in the openness of wind where who I appear
to be and who I am are one. Over there, near
to the oneness I can, here, only trace
like the fleeting forms of clouds the clouds chase,
there I am—still. And me. And I can hear,
clearly, words of grace that fill me, completely,
like water in an open vase. I’m not
ready, Lord, but want to be; want to trust
that you have formed me, Lord, that you have taught
me; that your love alone will complete me;
that there is life between and beyond dust and dust.

57

We eat his sacred body, living food.
It is the only living food on earth.
Not food in a state of dying or death,
or food that dies in me, having been good.
But living food, living in me, ark in flood
leading from life to life, from birth to birth.
He gave us himself in the flesh, his worth
made ours; but the proud mind thought it crude
that we should eat our God. What the humble heart
knows is that this living food, taken within,
transforms the dying body into life,
bit by bit; we are changed, become what we eat,
and so are freed from death, from pain, from sin,
from every fleeting form of fear and strife.

58

Reverence holds me back, but great love urges
me on to take my God under my poor
roof, unworthy though I am; and I adore
him in the Holy Sacrament, where faith surges
beyond sense, and the unbelieving mind purges
itself of its disbelief. I stand by the door,
Lord, on the infinite threshold of hope, where
love is, and where what is outside merges
with what is within. You become part of me,
and, slowly, the boundary between you
and me begins to dissolve till we see
one another face to face. My God, it's too
much to imagine, almost too good to be
true, like the sky in its impossible blue.

59

Perhaps it will appear to some that my
talking of those invisible things
is not entirely healthy, that it brings
to mind things distant and hidden by
things nearer to hand. Do we wonder why
poetry is dying? What poet sings
anymore of God, or of the soul, soars on wings
of celestial hope? Oh God, could you but untie
the hard knots that bind my tongue, I would praise
you with every word in me that would speak
truly, trusting that if I speak truly,
I should follow you and your humble ways
into poverty and obscurity, newly
made in your image, patient, mild and meek.

60

Return to me, O thou pure, clear, first love;
where have you gone, and how did you go?
Did you escape like sweat from the skin, no
sound but only a silent shimmer to prove
your going? I felt you once, felt the move
of the mover in my veins; and I know
that you were true. But then came the first blow,
followed by another, violent shove
of sin, mine, others; and it broke something, broke
me. Numbness of injury left me less
feeling than before. What would it take
to find you again? Or is first love a spoke
in the restless wheels of being which press
on, beyond this, to where none can break?

61

He languished in longing for our love. It
hurts to love and be unloved, to know and
be unknown, hurts even God. He could bend
the waves, the trees, the wind to his will, but
not our love, which bending or being bent
is broken. What breaks love, to the bitter end,
is pride, which is everywhere, always, like sand,
its abrasive, inescapable grit.
So he came for us, to show us the way
to him, the way to love, for we, too, were
languishing in longing for a love we
knew then only in part. He came to say
that humility is the only cure,
humility, humility, humility.

62

I love you, Lord, in loving distance, the way
the woman loved you who only touched your
hem; you healed, did not rebuke, her; nor
did you fault her leaving when she left. Your ray
reaches and warms us like the sun, whose day
is with us only half the time; but were
it not for your steadfast heat, which we wear
like a mantle about the chest, we'd cry
like Dante's Satan in a frozen pool
of our own making. My God, I don't know
why there are two kinds of distance, one
which drives away, the other which draws near;
only I know we can't look at the sun
directly, however strong the pull.

63

My joyous hope renews itself already,
a hope I had relinquished and allowed
to fade, of traveling beyond the crowd
out into the solitary blue, steady
in the face of every danger, ready
(ready!) for whatever comes. I vowed
long ago that I would not die, as the proud
do, in fear; that I would not be greedy
for life but thirsty for the truth. And then
life got the best of me, and I forgot
how to hold on to what matters. Let us go,
like the first four faithful fishermen,
who sailed on the face of the deep and fought
against fear to find faith, which led them home.

64

My soul proclaims the greatness of the Lord
is how she began her perfect, humble song.
And every word that flowed over her humble tongue
sounded like gentle, clear water poured
by grace over the stones of us, endured
patiently as, over time, our hard hearts are worn
smooth. Pray, our Blessed Mother, pray it won't be long
before our broken hearts and bodies turn toward
your son coming in glory on a bright cloud.
Make us new, Mother, make us worthy; make
us like you, put your sweet song in our hearts.
Lift up the lowly, scatter the proud;
let the love of you be our perpetual charts
across these final waters, where we wake.

65

I fight with wild beasts, by land and by sea, by
night and by day, he wrote en route to Rome
where he was thrown to lions. He would have come
without the chains, so glad was he to die
a martyr. And on the way he wrote to try,
in words soon sealed with blood, to give form
to his love for Holy Mother Church, his home.
He called her Catholic. He called us all to fly
in perfect unity, the way flocks of birds
move seamlessly through the sky, shifting
in fantastic unison, as though they
form a single fine fabric drifting
lightly on the wind. St. Ignatius, make my words
like yours; help me fight wild beasts night and day.

I wish I could see clearly through the senses,
the way the light here sometimes rarefies
the air; and like corrected vision, clarifies
a world lacking in distinction. These lenses,
for the poet, make meaning real, are the tenses
of creation; and Being verifies,
in every way it is, that we should care, if wise;
if we want to know what lies beyond our glances
in the places we're afraid to look. Christ came,
our light, it's true; but he came here in the flesh.
Not as spirit only, but as man, who
felt, and wept, and bled. The senses aren't to blame
when we fall, but the weakened will, which too
often distorts our way of seeing in a flash.

67

At midday, along the way, O king,
I saw a light brighter than the sun;
it washed over me like a wild spring rain,
and brought to life and changed my everything.
I've not gone mad with too much learning,
though I have learned much, and long. I tried to run
hard in the way of truth, but I was wrong.
I was wrong, O king; but now I bring
before you the fruits of being humbled
on my way. He came to me, the Truth, said,
"I am Jesus, whom thou persecutest; get up
now, and stand on your feet." So I did
and stand here now with words of truth on my lips,
to say I found the truth only when I stumbled.

68

Opening wide your arms upon the cross
and your blessed and pure wounds, O Lord, you
opened the heavens and limbo; and through
this self-sacrificing openness,
you gave us peace amidst pain and loss;
for you became a living portal to
your own sweet kingdom, which we can sense, and do,
when this world's cruel waves threaten to toss
us into an unforgiving sea.
Your kindness, Lord, calms our anxieties
the way your outstretched hand stilled the raging
sea; and amidst the cruel varieties
of hurt this life besets us with, like weather, we
need your kindness, Lord, to heal our graceless aging.

69

I have my eye fixed firmly upon the true end
of life's journey, but I'm not ready to die.
I'm like a house being readied by
the sea, not quite in order for a friend;
but I want to be, Lord, when you send
your angel over me. Let me cry
tears of love, make them strands of pearls and tie
them, softly, about my neck. Let me spend
what days remain in the elegant longing
of one who knows her lover comes, who loves
and is loved. Let it be like this, Lord, like
a joyful reunion in which the past lives,
fully present and purified, lingering
in the sweetness of a single, loving look.

70

Paul and Dionysius were the fertile crescent
of the early church, soil into which seeds
of humble truth were sewn, where proud weeds
might have choked them out, but didn't. Wasn't
it a miracle to find them present
in their search for truth so fully that their needs
were wholly set aside; and their words and deeds,
the substance of their thought, changed to such an extent
that they became one with the truth they sought?
How many of us could say the same?
My God, whose loving and merciful truth brought
me out of confusion and despair, who came
to fetch me when I was lost, make my ship taut
like theirs, fully sanctified and free of blame.

71

If the sweetness of heaven could still be seen
pouring from its living font pure grace
into the gentle heart, perhaps we could face
with clarity and courage those who have been
forgotten by the world. For there are some
who run from riches, honor, praise, who chase
after a different kind of treasure, whose race
is one of faith and not of wealth. They mean
to leave this world in conditions not better
than our Lord. Lord God, let me walk barefoot
and drunk with love, bearing my cross, overjoyed,
up the steep mountain of learning to care; put
your sweet words in my mouth, let them not taste bitter;
let me find in loving death life unalloyed.

72

Light intellectual replete with love
Love of the good replete with ecstasy
are the ecstatic lines in Canto 30
which descend from Dante's heaven like a dove
and light gently on truth, its loving worth to prove.
They reach my tired mind like a remedy,
like a promise that what I am here pressed to see
will unfurl eternally in the world above
like a wave without end on an endless shore.
The light fell softly on the grass tonight
and filled me with a gentle peace, as lungs feel
filled with breath. Although my aging sight
begins to fail, and I am injured more, and more,
I know there is a place ahead to see and heal.

73

O splendor of God, give me the power
to say how I saw it, ringed about with peace;
your light like a sun that never sets; pace
of movement like a perfect walk; shower
of grace like rain through sunlight where what is lower
is watered and drawn upward, and the rain prays
as it falls like a string of beads the fingers press,
and the soul opens like a willing flower.
I think sometimes if I could slow my seeing
to follow the droplets in their merciful fall,
to articulate water, light and air
in loving descent to Mother Earth, the wall
between me and the bountiful dream I desire
would give way, and I would walk the hills of being.

74

The invisible radiates out through
the visible, the way light pours out
from Christ's five wounds, which Thomas, in his doubt,
had to touch. And Christ rebukes him as one who knew
by unfeeling fact alone, who confronts the true,
demanding proof; because the beating heart
of being beats within, does not shout
its presence to the world; and yet to
one with ears to hear, its rhythm is everywhere.
What need have we to poke and prod, to peel
back the petals of the flower, when
emanating from everything, like air
from earth's surface, is the bright blue apparent
faith turning in the dark space of the real?

75

Humility is endless is the line
in Eliot that ripples outward as
from a small stone cast in an infinite pond. Was
it something of this sense that stood alone
for Colonna, too, made humility the spine
of all the virtues, the *sine qua non* that is,
and was, and is to come? It was his
gift to us, from birth to death; it was the sign
that shone in the small star and in the pale
tree; it was the substance of the love that stripped
him naked, bound him with cords, and led him
to the death that brought the whole world life. If I fail,
Lord, let me fail humbly; don't let the light grow dim
which shone most brightly when you fell, and hurt, and wept.

76

If, in this cold dark night, the door opens
to let the cruel wind in, the delicate inner
fire could go out. But faced with a stronger
flame, the same wind fuels the fire where hope ends
for the weaker. I don't know how it happens
that the senses drag the unwitting sinner
down, lead the lost soul onto thin and thinner
ice; while at the same time sensual hope sends
the searching soul, like wind under wings, toward
the source of that original fire arising
out of the emptiness. There's hope through the senses—
the new earth felt in the glory of the old,
passionate love for the firelit horizon,
truth expressed in weathered moods and tenses.

77

Our Lord conquered death with his heart alone.
His hidden heart, so full of love the blind
world couldn't see; he poured it out in death, blood
and water flowed like ink. Written in red lines
flowing from head, heart, hands and feet, he won
the battle against his enemies by
wounds not given, but received. Behind
the brokenness, in the simple words, "It is done,"
the wounded heart burned with a love so bright
no mortal eye could bear it. O God my
wounded God, let it be love that leads me
on; let these words flow from my wounds the way
blood flowed from yours; let what is hidden from sight
be known to the heart, that my love might flow freely.

78

To help us fix our eyes upon him, God gave
us a book; words like stars that can, when read with care,
help lead us home. Because our small minds can't bear
the brightness of its light, God gave us brave
priests and doctors to help us learn to love
in thought, deed and word. And if the bright flare
of the book was not enough, God dared
to send us the Word made flesh, that we might have
a vision of the living Word, of the law
not written upon paper, but upon the heart.
The book did not die with Christ but lives in him.
Neither learning nor sense is the fatal flaw,
only that which turns toward itself as source and end
and loses, like the dark side of the moon, all heat.

79

I cannot say, O my sweet comfort, that the place
is not opportune, the moment or the hour
for loving you better, for learning to hear,
for perfecting my will by the power of grace
or for sinking softly into that sweet space
from which all that is good and true in our
broken world flows. If it is not the hour,
it is because the hour is not within me; here
and now are always and only the way to change.
Yet I know that there is leeway in a life,
that sometimes wind and wave push us toward strange
shores against our will; but sanctification lifts
us like ocean swell over a long, wide range
until nothing but love of you is left.

80

God's loving and merciful eye has not seen
nor will see, but sees eternally; who I am,
have been, will be, is already known to him.
So then why do I remain closed in
upon myself, like a flower clenching
its petals tight around its center, hemmed
in by cold fear, unwilling to turn from
the winter of my discontent toward the green
fields of God's forgiving sun? Unfold me,
Lord; let me be not afraid; let every petal
unfurl fully that I might become who
I am, in the openness you've made me to be.
Let me not droop and fall, fold and settle,
having never let your bright warm sun break through.

81

I wish my mortal ear was closed and deaf
so that with a strong and concentrated mind
I could hear the clear celestial song, and find
in its living harmony, in the sweet puff
of wind that moves from chord to chord like a leaf
floating gracefully on water, the kind
of peace that here only silence brings. We're bound
in time to drop the perfect rhythm, to go off
key, to lose our attention to the good.
In our imperfect music, we hear
the hint of heaven, but it flashes and is gone
like a sparkle of sunlight on water. Would
the wind sing a different, sustaining song
if we could listen? Lord, open our ears.

82

He made his mother immaculate.
Lovingly he kept that beautiful crystal
always whole and sheltered in his palm. And all
will be well, for this kind God above all set
before his lost children the consummate
comfort, mother of infinite patience and all
tenderness, the one without whom the whole
world feels wrong. She is our shelter, our safety net,
our refuge from the storm; hers is the gentle
touch that relieves every anxiety. Mother
Eternal, make my heart as simple as a small
child; wrap me in your protective mantle;
pick me up and wipe my tears when I fall;
help me love those I meet as sister and brother.

83

Catherine of Alexandria, my bold
patron saint, resolved in truth and bound
to the word as to the wheel; my heart pounds
with the passion of your learning, and I hold
to the great gift of it, to the glimmering gold
of your purified mind, to the pure sound
of your clear voice, to the hope of your crowned
victory shining down on me in this cruel, cold
world. You stood for truth against every lie,
and it led you, gladly, to your death; and then
the angels came and carried your body on high,
to a place on earth marked with heaven,
so you could rest and bear witness on Mt. Sinai
to the gift of the word where God himself had written.

84

In the long oblivion of a lifetime, spread
out like a wide sea between the shores
of birth and death, waves rising and falling like years,
the past gathers darkness like a storm; speed
of wind and wave intensifies, heart and head
oppose one another like current and wind—wars
waged in the soul beneath the still stars.
But in the midst, Christ emerged from sleep, said
"Be still," and all was still. The past, the storm, is gone.
Not without effort we navigate darkness
and pain; not without guilt and sorrow we
confront our sin. But the sheer force of it, the starkness
of life without him, gives way, wind and wave atone,
and we sail calm waters of grace in ecstasy.

85

I see the clear and pure truth shrouded
in a thousand ornate veils, and with a thousand
false sparks of pity, I see a dozen
false faces flash across the true face, crowded
with the flickering uncertainties of a muddied
faith. I hear a thousand false sirens seasoned
in the art of fatal distraction; all reasoned
love is gone. Cursed century, where what is lauded
turns immediately to dust; where honor, life,
time, and riches appear to the eye yet
are absent in the heart. My God, what worth
is worth if not eternal? The brown oak leaf
hisses in the wind, clinging to the average north,
singing its average song of lust and fret.

86

Fleeing the cruel reign of Herod, the noble kings,
through high divine reason outside their blind
human understanding, went out to find,
beyond their native kingdom, the true path which brings
peace. So, too, we should flee the proud and godless things
of this vain world and seek a different kind
of kingdom, that bright true light shining behind
the shadows, the one of which the poet sings.
And when we seek out our own eternal region
along this other more lonely and more lovely
way, when we venture beyond the known in all
humility, one star shines out from the legion
of small stars to guide us as we heed the call
to a courageous faith more lovely and more lively.

87

At the terrible thought of Christ on the cross, waves
of tears should rise up from our shores like wild
horses shying at the sight; and the weak-willed
soul should fall before the God who saves
by bearing its terrible weight, who moves
the unmoved world with the gift of a child
sent to show us his kind face, merciful and mild.
He sent his son, his manner as mild as the dove's;
and our violent hearts, our sins like nails, drove
him to an end no peaceful mind could ever
comprehend. He came to us in our exile
to open a door where we built a wall;
to walk through is to walk the way of love,
to embrace the life-giving cross as lover.

88

Tell me, light of the world and radiant glory
of the sky, now that you know the sweet taste
of life after death, having bravely faced
the cross, what virtue sustained you in your weary
hours hanging in pain from three nails? The hurry
of this indifferent world wounds you; the waste
of a life spent chasing after vain things chased
when you are the only part of our story
that leads anywhere. Our Christ, our crucified,
our hope in the end, how did you bear
the cross and the cruel indifference that nailed
you there? In my heart, I heard him say, "I died
for love of you, love held me there, where not to care
is the unhealing wound of having failed."

89

Today, in my thoughts, I see beneath the hand
of John the Baptist the Son of God washing
himself in the sacred river, not wishing
thereby to cleanse himself, but as God planned,
to purify the race of man. I see him stand
in the water, white dove descending, blessing
from above his humble act. Why are we pushing
him away, day by day, in this polluted land,
compelled by a mad and impure lust
to pollute ourselves again, and then, corrupted,
distance ourselves with loathing from his life-giving
spring? My God, without you we are lost.
Make us like your son, humble, pure, adopted
into the sacred and hopeful art of living.

90

If our weak virtue cannot fly straight
toward the first cause, let it at least
observe itself and admit that it is lost,
that it cannot bear the tremendous weight
of being entrapped in so much sin. All the hate
and bitterness, resentment and regret, lust
turned to hurt and shame; all this and more will be loosed
in heaven for the humble heart, and the sweet gate
of Being will be opened. Our Lord longs
to unburden us, but we have to want
to be unburdened; then, wanting this sweet
unburdening, our Lord leads us to his sweet font
of mercy, where we are given a new voice, complete
and true, with which to sing him new and better songs.

91

The alchemy of grace in the heart turns
the lead of sin into pure, untarnished gold;
it's the only alchemy, fresh and bold,
of any consequence. For the rest, the world learns
slowly; and the avaricious heart burns
with the wrong fire; and what is daily sold
as vital turns to nothing; and all that Christ told
us is forgotten. My God, make me one who yearns
for the right thing; let me care not for anything
not from you. I want to burn with your fire
alone, to feel the turn in me from stone
to flesh, to leave this cold world with nothing
but what remains. Let me burn on your holy pyre,
till it's gone, all that is unworthy, poorly done.

92

If it should ever rain down money,
we would see a frenzied gathering of this short-
lived treasure, gone as fast as dew; we'd abort
all human reason, feud and hoard every penny
when right here daily, under God's sunny
blue, under gray, under cloud, in every sort
of weather, God's grace rains down into the heart
open to receive it. Today the willing many
will for money, turning from his eternal shower
of infinite treasure; money is the only
merit, and the currencies of love and faith
are obsolete. My God, grant me the power
to be poor to men but rich to you; lonely
though the path be, for comfort give me truth.

93

I see the Holy Spirit hovering with face
aflame, ready to set fire to the underbrush
of Holy Mother Church; because the over-lush
forest must occasionally be burned in case
the wildfire comes and in a great fiery race
burns the whole thing down. This is the push
of the true reformer, to set fire to the bush
without taking down the forest; to let grace
control the burn and save the trees. But when
the Holy Spirit's fire is suppressed, wild
heresy rages, sweeping up into flames ten
times the size, leaping and running strong-willed
wherever it pleases; and when it's done,
all the trees are gone, and the earth is black and soiled.

94

This is not the humble dwelling, nor these
the loving arms of your holy Mother, nor
the shepherds, nor the angelic choir,
nor the three wise kings on their royal knees,
nor the sweet affection of Simeon, whose
Nunc dimittis is the humble door
opening onto peaceful death. I am too poor
of spirit, Lord, to embody any of those
graces; yet you are here, with me, looking
up at me with bright, gentle, trusting eyes
like a baby newly born; and like a new
mother, I feel unworthy and afraid. But waking
into a bright new morning, new because of you,
I feel the hopeful clarity of twilit skies.

95

Pure Virgin, whose beautiful light, during your
toilsome earthly life, kept your lovely eyes
serene and contented, whose earthly skies
were always full of hope, whose humble door
was always open; you dwelt, happily, poor
in the eyes of the world, sharing the sweet highs
and most sorrowful lows of the Son of Man; his sighs
were yours, his pain; yet the hurtful world never wore
you down, for your joy was like the quiet snow
carefully everywhere descending, bringing
to the hurried world an otherworldly stillness.
Gentle Mother, let your joy rest on me, singing
quiet songs of peace; let the branches of my days bow
low, replete with your otherworldly fullness.

96

Blessed is the soul that scorns all worldly pleasure
in this brief, troubled stay on earth; and blessed
is the soul that feels the world, whose heart is pressed
like a leaf between blocks to gain the sacred treasure
of essential oils wrung. It's a different measure
to weigh the poet, and the saint whose rest
came through defiance of the senses, whose soul confessed
hatred of the world; where this painful fissure,
for the poet, between the maker and the made,
is a fault line in the feeling heart that shakes,
when it slips, the stable senses, which, when good, sense
in the world the heft of God. All it takes
is to feel, in the still point, the eternal dance
of body, mind and soul together lightly weighed.

97

I cannot now say: my faith is like a rock
which, when the savage sea rages, turns its strong
face to the fury and sends the proud wave, wrong
in its vicious attacks, retreating back
upon itself. That is not my faith. I walk,
head bowed low, softly with a quiet song, along
the jagged shore where all the bits of things belong,
the broken shells and tangled seaweed by the dock
which reaches only so far into the sea.
My faith is small and fragile, like a piece of glass;
and if I have a hope in it, it is this:
that the waves which daily crash will pass
their violent waters over me, and I will be
worn wholly smooth beneath their whitened hiss.

98

The sight of lively water tumbling down
or of a perfect wave finding its form
moves us and makes us feel that nature's term
is too subtle for mere human noun.
But the need for her ecstatic language to be known
makes us reach after the place it's coming from,
hoping to find in her eloquent, firm
voice a way to speak as clearly as the dawn.
Possibly we fail; possibly our words
are but a record of our failure. But if
it is a failure, like the storm, then let its
dissipation scatter like a flock of birds,
vital energies which fill the sky in fits
and starts, but well beyond the sharp edge of the cliff.

99

I, burdened by my years, am frozen here.
Too many cold and hurtful words have stilled
my heart. But you, my sons and daughters, filled
with hope and faith and not with servile fear,
all aflame with love of wind and weather, your
swift hearts will gather humbly, rise and build,
like a milk-white golden storm, elegant and bold,
finding the thunderous voice of spring year after year.
What is it in this striking movement of the sky
that brings real hope along with the kind
of fear that leads to wisdom, makes us know
the sterile air won't have the final word? I
pray for you, my children, rain down hard; find
in strength of wind and rain the way and grace to grow.

100

Eternal moon, when your mortal light was placed
between the true sun and our eyes, you didn't mar
his image; rather, you offered us a mirror
in which to gaze upon his divine light. Faced
with the dense black veil of original sin, you laced
your sweet veil of prayer and light over us; married
to the truth, you transformed our sinful nature more
and more, making what was dark and heavy, what was waste
and void, into a heavenly body radiant
and light. With the clarity that you take from him,
the darkness of night is banished, and your calm, silk
light tempers his heat; riding the gradient
invisible of your silver light, our dim
souls grow bright, nurtured by your pure milk.

101

I see your net so laden with weeds and mud,
Peter, that if some wave breaks over it, it may
be torn, endangering your boat; for it can't ply
the waters, light and free, when it is so weighed
down that it sails the turbulent flood
in grave danger. Still, what is this mad way
that senses in the foul mood of the sea, in its high
fury, a better ally than the boat? Who would
rather leap into the sea than cut the net?
Let us reform it from within, with tightened grip,
beginning with ourselves; neither pride nor
anger, but only grace, will help us shed our weight.
We have Christ himself on board; therefore,
let us not, ever, abandon ship.

102

If I often fail to take up the file
of good sense to polish or erase my rough,
uncultivated verses, it's because my tough
way is not to care what others think, to accept the trial
of indifference or contempt or praise, while
also trying to refuse the thought that it's enough
if my verses go on living after my death. This trough
is wide and deep in which to fall. The mile
leading to the end is long and lonely.
There is only this: I write because I must.
The way the fire sparks. If this divine fire
which through its mercy inflames my mind, should entrust
these humble sparks to one gentle heart whose fear
thus melts away, I would be immeasurably blessed.

103

Lord, receive my heart; it's all I have to give.
I fear sometimes I write from habit and not
from the fire of love of you. If I forgot
something along the way, Lord, forgive me. I live
in and through the word which lives in love
and silence. My Lord, for years I fought
the demons of doubt and despair, sought
to bribe my way onto another path; I'd leave
and come back again, worried that everything I'd write
would only do harm. If these words do harm, Father
forgive me. But if they may be of service, Lord,
I pray they keep the lightness of a feather
and fly to you, shining with the brightness of your light
and the eternal sharpness of your fiery sword.

INDEX OF FIRST LINES

Printed in the USA
CPSIA information can be obtained
at www.ICGtesting.com
JSHW031351020923
47379JS00005B/18

9 781949 497038